Science in a flash

Rocks

Georgia
Amson-Bradshaw

W
FRANKLIN WATTS
LONDON·SYDNEY

Franklin Watts
First published in Great Britain in 2017 by The Watts Publishing Group

Copyright © The Watts Publishing Group 2017

 Produced for Franklin Watts by
White-Thomson Publishing Ltd
www.wtpub.co.uk

Credits
Series Editor: Georgia Amson-Bradshaw
Series Designer: Rocket Design (East Anglia) Ltd

Images from Shutterstock.com: Albert Russ 4bl, Imageman 5tl, Tyler Boyes 5tr,
Johan Swanepoel 6bl, Mopic 7c, snapgalleria 8bl, vvoe 8br, vilax 9bl, vvoe 9tr, corlaffra 10b, holbox 11cr,
farbled 13br, psynovec 16br, Leene 16cl, Arlene Treiber Waller 17bl, Vladimir Melnik 17t, hanohiki 17br,
Christian Musat 19c, Kamira 19br, Imfoto 24l, Preobrajenskiy 26bl, Taveesak Pansang 26br, Santi Rodriguez
26t, Alexander Donchev 27c, IrinaK 27t
Illustrations from wikicommons: Alexander Van Driessche 4t, Kotivalo 27b
Illustrations by Steve Evans: 4br, 5b, 7tr, 7bl, 11r, 13l, 12c, 13c, 15, 21, 23
All design elements from Shutterstock.

Every attempt has been made to clear copyright. Should there be any inadvertent omission
please apply to the publisher for rectification.

HB ISBN 978 1 4451 5278 3
PB ISBN 978 1 4451 5279 0

Printed in China

Franklin Watts
An imprint of
Hachette Children's Group
Part of The Watts Publishing Group
Carmelite House
50 Victoria Embankment
London EC4Y 0DZ

An Hachette UK Company
www.hachette.co.uk

www.franklinwatts.co.uk

In this book you'll see some words shown in **bold**. These are described on the glossary page at the back of the book.

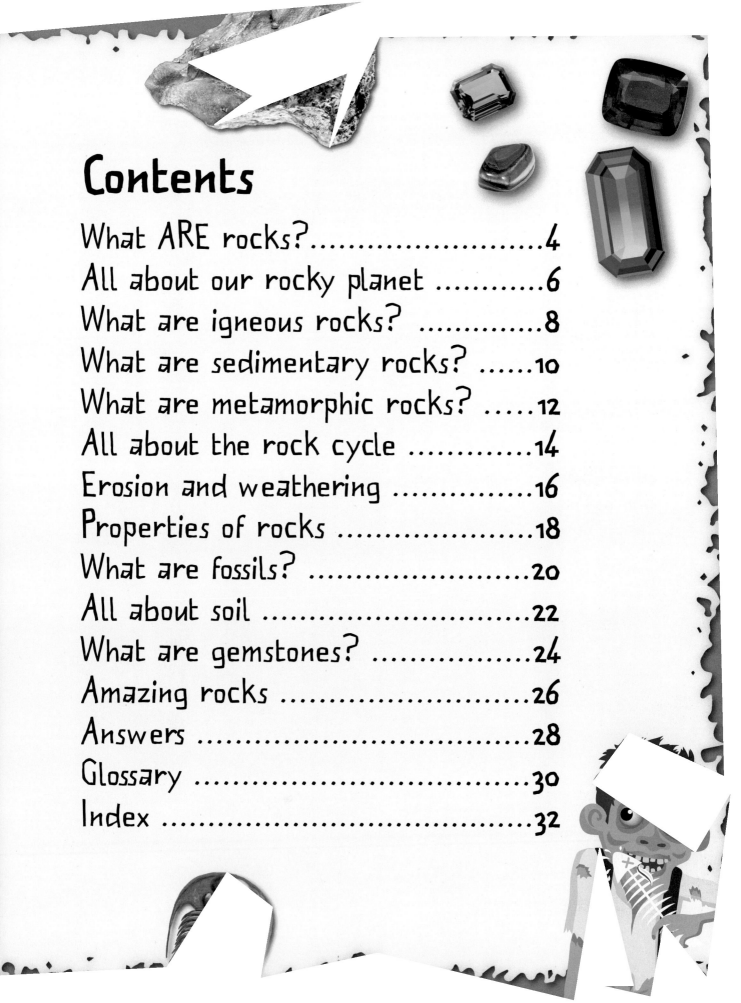

Contents

WHAT ARE ROCKS?

Rocks are naturally occurring solids made up of minerals.

What's the difference between a **rock** and a **mineral**? Minerals are solid substances that are made up of the same thing all the way through. Rocks are usually made up of lots of different types of mineral.

Cool crystals

All minerals have a '**crystal** structure'. What's that? Well, everything in the world is made of **atoms**. In many materials the atoms are arranged in an irregular, higgledy-piggledy way. Having a crystal structure means the atoms are arranged in a tidy, ordered pattern. This means lumps of mineral naturally come in crystal shapes.

Mineral crystals can grow to enormous sizes, like in Mexico's 'Cave of Crystals'.

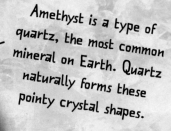

Amethyst is a type of quartz, the most common mineral on Earth. Quartz naturally forms these pointy crystal shapes.

Minerals for dinner?

Humans need tiny amounts of some minerals in their diets to stay healthy. Milk contains the mineral calcium, which we need to grow our bones.

It's MINERALS you need, not rocks!

The different minerals in this piece of polished granite can be clearly seen.

In this piece of slate the different minerals can't be seen by the naked eye.

Rockin' rocks

Rocks are made up of different minerals mixed together. Sometimes the grains of different minerals can be easily seen, like in a piece of granite. Rocks come in three types, according to how the rock was made. These three types are **sedimentary**, **igneous** and **metamorphic**.

Read about the three types of rock on pages 8–13.

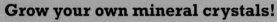

Give it a go!

Grow your own mineral crystals!

You will need a measuring jug, Epsom salt (available in chemists), a saucepan, hot water, a spoon, food colouring and a glass jar.

Mix a quarter of a jug of hot water with half a jug of Epsom salt in the saucepan. Stir for five minutes until the salt is completely dissolved and the water is clear.

Ask an adult to heat the water further if the salt won't fully dissolve.

Add a few drops of food colouring and stir. Pour the mixture into the jar and leave it in the fridge overnight.

In the morning, pour away the extra liquid in the jar. You should have pretty crystals left behind. Find out what has happened on page 28.

All about our rocky planet

Our Earth is a big ball of rocks and minerals floating through space.

Four and a half billion years ago, there was no Sun or Earth as we know them now, just a lot of dust and gas swirling around in space. The dust and gases were pulled together by gravity, and eventually formed into the Sun and the planets, including Earth.

PLANET EARTH
Solidifying in process – come back in four billion years.

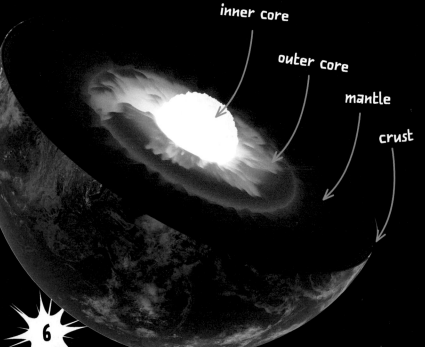

inner core

outer core

mantle

crust

Earth's birth

In the beginning, the Earth was molten rock. The **atmosphere** was dark and poisonous – not the kind of place you'd want to visit! Eventually the Earth cooled down, and the surface solidified into the **crust**. Our Earth now has several layers, including the crust, the **mantle** and the outer and inner **core**.

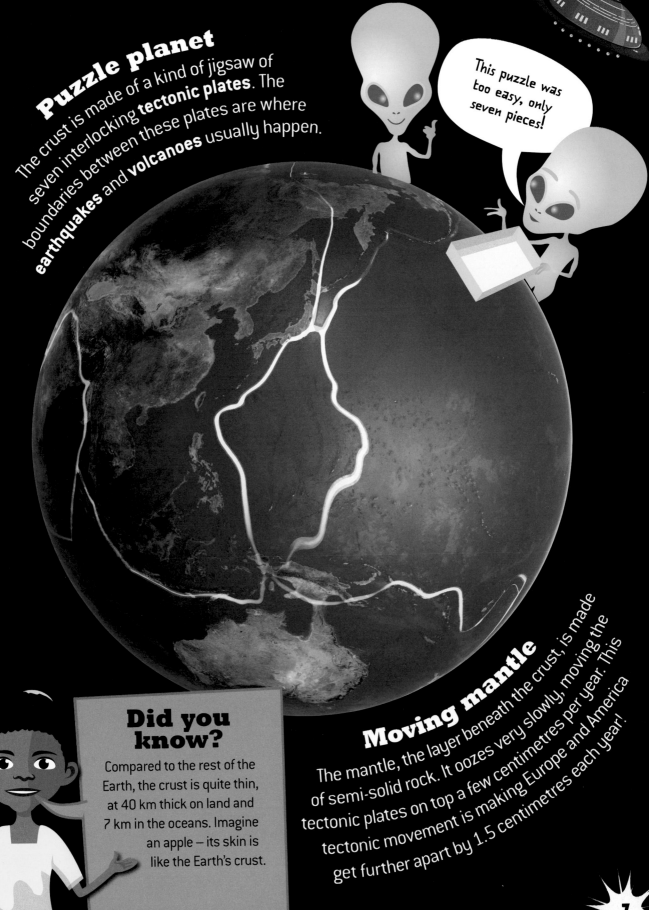

Puzzle planet

The crust is made of a kind of jigsaw of seven interlocking **tectonic plates**. The boundaries between these plates are where **earthquakes** and **volcanoes** usually happen.

This puzzle was too easy, only seven pieces!

Did you know?

Compared to the rest of the Earth, the crust is quite thin, at 40 km thick on land and 7 km in the oceans. Imagine an apple – its skin is like the Earth's crust.

Moving mantle

The mantle, the layer beneath the crust, is made of semi-solid rock. It oozes very slowly, moving the tectonic plates on top a few centimetres per year. This tectonic movement is making Europe and America get further apart by 1.5 centimetres each year!

What are igneous rocks?

Igneous rocks are made when molten rock cools into a solid.

In places deep underground, there is incredibly hot molten rock. When this cools into a solid it forms igneous rock. Igneous rock can be made of many different minerals. How these minerals cool also affects what type of rock is created.

Cool on the surface

Igneous rocks that are made when **lava** from volcanoes cools on the surface of the Earth are called **extrusive**. Above ground, lava cools quickly and doesn't have time to form crystals. Basalt and obsidian are extrusive igneous rocks.

Shiny black obsidian is made from lava that has cooled very fast.

Cool inside

When molten rock solidifies underground, it is called **intrusive**. It cools more slowly, so big crystals can form. Granite is an intrusive igneous rock.

During explosive volcanic eruptions, blobs of molten rock get spurted into the air. They cool as they fly through the air making rock missiles called **lava bombs**.

POP QUIZ!

Diorite is an igneous rock with big, visible crystals. Do you think it is:

a) an intrusive igneous rock

b) an extrusive igneous rock?

Answer on page 28.

Great granite

The igneous rock granite is the type of rock that makes up the bulk of Earth's continental crust – the parts of the crust that are not under the oceans.

Float like a ... stone?

Did you know there is a type of rock that floats? Pumice is an igneous rock that is full of air bubbles. It is made when gas-filled lava comes out of a volcano.

Nice beach, shame about the lava bombs.

What are **sedimentary** rocks?

Sedimentary rocks are formed by small bits of rock settling in layers.

Rocks are constantly being ground down by the water or wind, creating tiny fragments of rock. These bits get washed into lakes or the ocean, where they settle on the bottom and mix with other minerals and seashells. We call this mixture **sediment**. Over thousands of years, the layers of sediment build up. The added weight starts to crush it all together, forming new sedimentary rocks.

fossilised ammonite

fossilised trilobite

Fossil spots

Sedimentary rocks are where we find **fossils**. The bodies of dead animals and plants stick in the sediment when it is soft. Over time more sediment builds up on top, and the bodies of the plants and animals become **fossilised**.

These sedimentary rocks are in Utah, USA.

Rock clocks

Sedimentary rocks are very interesting to **geologists** because the different layers reveal a picture of the Earth in the past. Geologists can tell if an area used to be a desert or an ocean, and fossils reveal what creatures lived in the area during each period.

Building with sand

The sedimentary rock sandstone is often used as a building material. It comes in many different colours, such as this red sandstone used to build the Red Fort in India.

Can you SQUASH a rock?

Rocks aren't always hard. One of the most useful sedimentary rocks is clay, a rock that is squidgy and sticky when wet. It can be shaped into all sorts of useful items and then baked solid.

FACT ATTACK

SCRUB SCRUB

You have probably used animal skeletons to clean your teeth ... yes really! It might sound gruesome, but chalk, a common ingredient in toothpaste, is a sedimentary rock made of the skeletons of tiny sea creatures that are too small to see with the naked eye.

WHAT ARE METAMORPHIC ROCKS?

Igneous and sedimentary rocks change into metamorphic rocks when they are heated and squeezed by powerful forces. Metamorphic rocks can change into different kinds of metamorphic rock, when heated or squeezed again.

Under pressure

The temperatures and pressure deep underground are hard for us to imagine. The conditions are so intense that they can change the appearance and chemical make-up of rock. When tectonic plates move together, mountains are created as the plates collide and buckle.

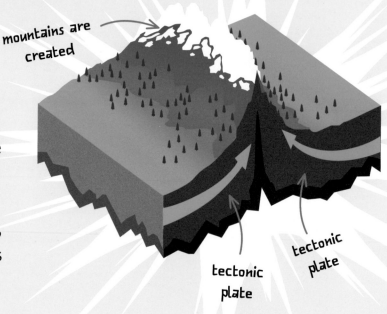

mountains are created

tectonic plate

tectonic plate

Hi, I'm Gneiss.

I'll be the judge of that!

Nice gneiss

The oldest rocks in the world are metamorphic rocks. Geologists have discovered that a type of metamorphic rock called gneiss (said like 'nice') in Canada is 4 billion years old.

Many marbles

Marble is a type of metamorphic rock created when limestone is heated to high temperatures. Because marble is easy to carve and polish, people use it to make statues and for decoration in buildings. A lot of marble is white, but it comes in many colours and patterns.

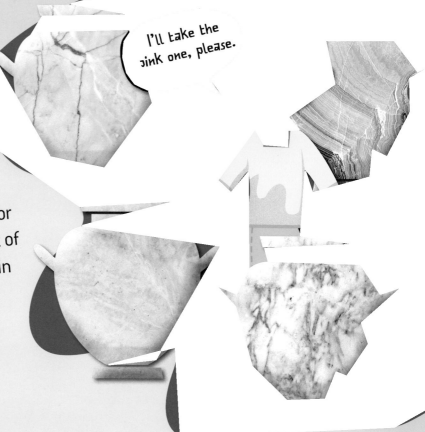

I'll take the pink one, please.

Congratulations, it's a marble!

Rock relatives

The original rock type that a metamorphic rock is made from is called the **parent rock**. For example, limestone is the parent rock of marble, and granite is the parent rock of gneiss. Read more about how rocks can change on pages 14 and 15.

FACT ATTACK

Most metamorphic rocks are formed over many thousands of years. But a fulgurite is a type of glassy rock made in a flash – literally! When a flash of lightning hits sand or some types of rock, it fuses the sand together into a knobbly mineral tube. Insta-rock!

All about the ROCK CYCLE

Rocks are constantly being recycled into new types of rock.

It's hard to imagine when you look at a mountain or a rocky landscape, but the rocks on our planet are constantly changing. Over millions of years, rocks are broken down and remade into new types of rock. This process is called the **rock cycle**.

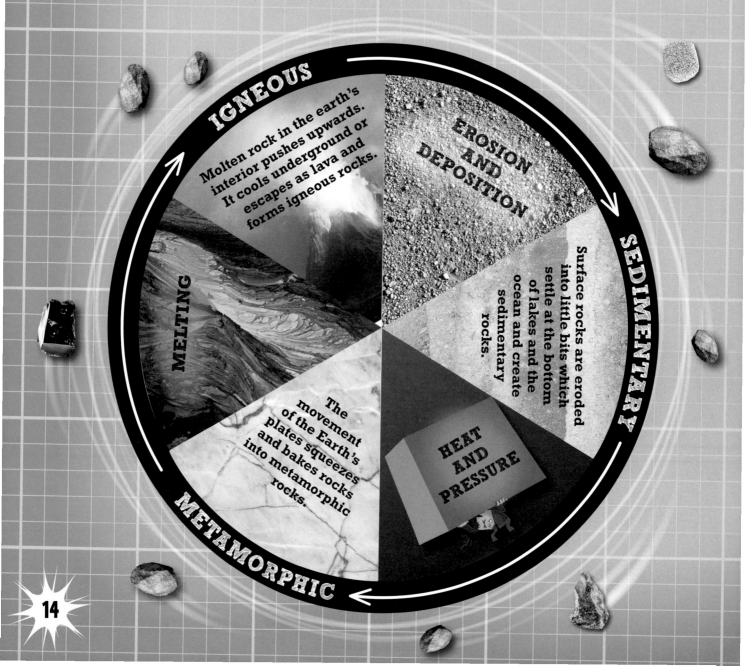

IGNEOUS

Molten rock in the earth's interior pushes upwards. It cools underground or escapes as lava and forms igneous rocks.

EROSION AND DEPOSITION

SEDIMENTARY

Surface rocks are eroded into little bits which settle at the bottom of lakes and the ocean and create sedimentary rocks.

MELTING

The movement of the Earth's plates squeezes and bakes rocks into metamorphic rocks.

HEAT AND PRESSURE

METAMORPHIC

Give it a go!

Understand the rock cycle better ... with chocolate! You'll need a large bar of chocolate, a glass bowl, a microwave, a cheese grater, an oven-proof dish, a handful of puffed rice, a handful of mini marshmallows, some baking paper, an oven and a spatula. Always ask an adult's permission before using the oven.

Step 1

Break your chocolate into small pieces, and put it in the glass bowl. Heat it in the microwave for 1 minute. Stir it. Keep heating for 15 seconds at a time until it is all melted. This is your lava!

Step 2

Pour your chocolate lava onto baking paper, and let it cool. This is your igneous rock.

Step 3

Grate your igneous chocolate rock to make 'sediment'. Put a layer of puffed rice in the oven-proof dish, then a layer of marshmallows, then top it with your layer of grated chocolate. It won't quite be solid, but these layers are your sedimentary rock.

Step 4

Pop the dish in the oven at 150°C. After a few minutes when it is hot and melted, fold and squish the mixture together and let it cool into a solid. This is your metamorphic rock. Unlike actual rock, it can be eaten when your experiment is over. Yum!

EROSION AND WEATHERING

Weathering breaks rocks down and erosion wears them away.

Even the hardest rocks don't last forever. They get ground down slowly over time in various different ways. **Erosion** and **weathering** can create amazing rock formations and are an important part of the rock cycle.

Heavy weather

Weathering is when a rock is broken down by heat from the weather or chemicals in rain. **Chemical weathering** is when **acidic rainwater** slowly dissolves rocks over time. This sort of weathering can often be seen on statues and carvings on buildings.

Feeling flaky

Water gets into cracks in rock. If the temperature drops and the water freezes, it can split the rock open because water expands as it freezes. But even without water, temperature changes can break rocks down. When rocks are repeatedly heated and cooled, they expand and then shrink, gradually cracking and flaking.

I think I'm cracking up!

Gone with the wind

Erosion is when pieces of rock are broken off and carried away. The wind is a big cause of erosion. Wind carries sand and other particles, and blasts them against rocks like sandpaper, grinding them away. Over time, the wind can create amazing rock sculptures.

POP QUIZ!

Which of these rocks do you think has been eroded by the wind, and which has been weathered by temperature changes?

Answer on page 28.

a

b

Properties of rocks

Rocks have different characteristics, making them useful for different things.

Not all rocks are alike. Some really are 'rock hard', whereas others are soft and crumbly. Rocks have different **properties** depending on the minerals they are made of, and how they are formed. We use different types of rocks for different jobs.

Soft rock

Chalk is a soft, crumbly rock. Its texture means it can be ground into a powder and used in cleaning products. In the past, it was used for writing on blackboards, but today, blackboard chalks are made of a mineral called gypsum.

HARD ROCK

Granite is a really tough rock. The way the mineral crystals are compacted together mean it is very strong, and it doesn't split easily. Granite is often used on buildings or for gravestones as it will last a long time.

Waterproof or water carrier?

We don't normally imagine rocks containing water, but some rocks can soak up water like a sponge. We call these sorts of rocks **permeable**. Sandstone is a permeable rock. Others don't soak up water, and we call those **impermeable**. Slate is impermeable. It is also hard, but can be split into thin sheets. This makes slate very useful for roof tiles.

Riddle me this!

Which type of metamorphic rock is used for decorations because it is easy to cut and polish, and comes in lots of different colours?

Answer on page 28.

FACT ATTACK

Flint is a hard rock that splits in any direction and makes a sharp edge. Because of these properties, early humans used flint to make some of the first tools.

I'm so bored, plea- move me out of this

19

For **palaeontologists**, fossils are an incredible snapshot of life on Earth in ancient times. Fossils are very special because the circumstances needed for a plant or animal to fossilise are quite rare. Almost all fossils are found in sedimentary rock.

Recipe for a fossil

Fossils are formed when a creature or a plant dies, and is quickly buried after death. This might be by sinking into mud, or being covered by sand in a sandstorm, or falling to the bottom of a lake or ocean and being covered with sediment.

Over time, more and more sediment covers the remains of the creature. The remains of the living thing decays very slowly.

At the same time as the body is decaying, it is being replaced by minerals which harden into rock. Eventually, a rock copy of the creature is left in place. This is why fossils look like rocks: it is because they ARE rocks!

Make a model fossil. You'll need some plasticine, a plastic container, shells or plastic toys, a mixing jug, a spoon, water and plaster of Paris.

Put the plasticine in the bottom of the plastic container so it makes a flat layer about 2 cm deep. Press the shells or plastic toys into the plasticine, then pull them out, so they leave an imprint.

Mix around two-thirds of a cup of plaster of Paris with one-third of a cup of water in the measuring jug. Stir it with a spoon until there are no lumps.

Pour the plaster of Paris into the plastic container, and let it dry for 24 hours. When the plaster is dry, remove it from the plastic container. You have a homemade fossil!

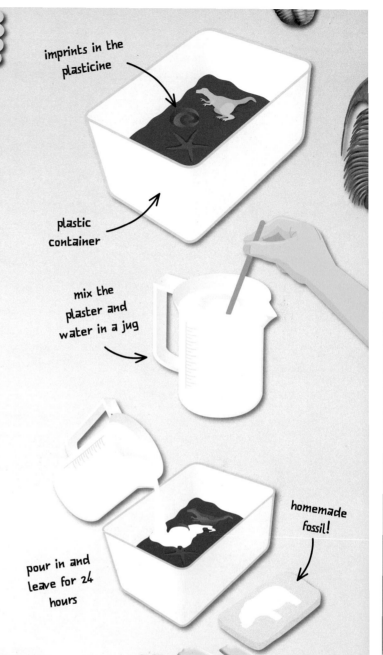

imprints in the plasticine

plastic container

mix the plaster and water in a jug

pour in and leave for 24 hours

homemade fossil!

Did you know?

Fossils can sometimes provide an action snapshot! Fossils have been found of dinosaurs that died and were buried in the middle of a fight and even while giving birth.

EYE SPY!

How many fossils can you count on these pages?

Answer on page 28.

All about soil

Soil is a mixture of tiny bits of rock and decayed plants.

Soil is a mixture of rocks, dead plant and animals remains, and lots of tiny bugs and **bacteria**. Sounds gross! But soil is very important. It's full of nutrients that plants need to grow and is essential to life on Earth.

So many soils

Soil doesn't just come in one variety. Soils are different from place to place, depending on the exact mixture of rocks and materials that they are made from. Sandy soils are quite dry and crumbly and don't hold a lot of water. Clay soils are denser and water doesn't pass through them so quickly.

ORGANIC LAYER: plant and animal matter.

TOP SOIL: mostly plant and animal matter mixed with some minerals.

Digging down

Soil is made of different layers, called **horizons**. Each layer contains different proportions of rock and plant and animal matter. The top layer has the most plant and animal matter and the deepest layers contain the most rock. The type of soil in a particular place depends on the type of rock that lies beneath it.

SUB SOIL: lots of rocks and minerals, a small amount of organic matter.

PARENTAL MATERIAL: eroded rocks.

BEDROCK: solid rock layer.

Did you know?

It takes a very long time for soil to form, up to 1,000 years for a depth of just two centimetres! Soil is essential to grow plants, which then support all other life on Earth. When plants are removed and soil is left bare, it can be washed away in a process called **soil erosion**.

Riddle me this!

Why do you think soil erosion is a problem for humans and animals?

Answer on page 29.

Give it a go!

See how removing plants from the landscape causes soil erosion in this experiment. You'll need a small potted plant, a small plant pot full of soil but no plant, two clear containers slightly larger than the pots, and some water.

Place your potted plant and your pot of soil into the two containers.

Pour equal amounts of water into your potted plant and your pot of soil. Watch how quickly the water passes through the two pots into the clear containers below. Compare how muddy the water is that has passed through. What do you notice?

potted plant

soil only

Water both pots, what can you see?

WHAT ARE GEMSTONES?

crystals that can
be cut and polished into pretty jewels.

There are around 3,000 types of mineral on Earth, but only about 130 of them form the pretty, colourful gems that people love ... and spend a lot of money on!

uncut or rough diamonds

cut diamonds

From rock to jewel

All jewels, including diamonds, rubies and emeralds, start out as roughly shaped, uncut minerals. By cutting and polishing the minerals, craftspeople can shape them into sparkling jewels.

Precious stones

How much a gem is worth depends on a few things, like how rare it is, how big and how clear it is. One of the most expensive gemstones ever sold is the octagon-shaped Oppenheimer Blue diamond which sold for £40 million in May 2016.

EYE SPY!

How many polished gems can you see on these pages?

Answer on page 29.

Transparent gems like diamonds are cut to have lots of **facets**, or sides. This makes light bounce around inside them so they sparkle.

diamond

emerald

ruby

Sapphires and rubies are actually the same mineral: corundum. The gems are called rubies if they are red and sapphires if blue.

sapphire

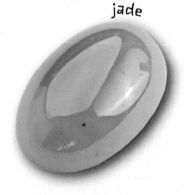

opal

turquoise

tiger's eye

jade

Some gems, like turquoise, are **opaque**. They often have strong colours from their chemical makeup.

amethyst

Precious stones are found all around the world. They are mined, or dug, out of the ground. In the USA, there are many privately-owned small mines where you can pay to search for gems in the rock.

lapis lazuli

rose quartz

In the past, people used ground-up minerals, like lapis lazuli, as paint pigments.

AMAZING ROCKS

Over time, rocks can be shaped into incredible formations.

Rocks change very slowly compared to human lifespans, but the processes of erosion and of **deposition** (bits of rock piling up in new places) can create crazy-looking natural sculptures.

Grown by water

Water passing through rocks can dissolve the minerals and carry them along with it. When the water drips from the ceiling to the floor in a cave, the minerals get deposited, creating weirdly shaped columns that hang from the ceiling and rise from the floor.

Cool caves

Caves often feature incredible natural rock sculptures in the shape of dangling stalactites and towering stalagmites.

POP QUIZ!

Which of these are stalactites and which are stalagmites?

Answer on page 29.

a

b

Nature's architect

Outside in the open air where rocks are exposed to the weather, erosion can create crazy rock formations. In the Arches National Park in the USA, the sandstone has eroded to leave natural arches or 'bridges'. In Cappadocia in Turkey, erosion has created strange 'fairy chimneys' with pointy roofs!

Arches National Park, USA

Wish you were here in Cappadocia!

Greetings from Kummakivi

Dropped rocks

Kummakivi, in Finland, is a huge boulder balancing on a stone beneath. Finnish folklore says it was put there by trolls, but geologists believe that was carried along by a glacier, and left behind when the ice melted.

And the answer is...

Page 5 **Give it a go:** As the mixture of water and Epsom salt cools and evaporates in the fridge, the atoms that make up the Epsom salt run into each other and naturally join together in a crystal structure.

Page 9 **Pop quiz:** The answer is **a**, diorite is an intrusive igneous rock. Intrusive igneous rocks cool slowly, which is what allows their large mineral crystals to form.

Page 17 **Pop quiz: a** has been eroded by the wind, and **b** has been weathered by temperature changes. The kind of weathering where the outer layers peel away after the rock is repeatedly heated and cooled is called onion-skin weathering, because the layers of the rock look like the layers of an onion.

Page 19 **Riddle me this:** The type of metamorphic rock that comes in many colours, and is often used for decorations is: **marble**.

Page 21 **Eye spy:** There are **9** fossils on pages 20–21.

Page 23

Riddle me this: Soil erosion is a problem for humans because when the layer of rich, fertile soil is washed away, it makes it harder to grow crops. Bare, thin soils are also more prone to flooding. Soil erosion is also bad for plants that need healthy, deep soils to grow in, and for the animals that rely on the plants.

Page 24

Eye spy: There are **34** polished gems on pages 24–25.

Page 26

Pop quiz: a shows stalactites and **b** shows stalagmites. You can remember it like this: stalacTites hang from the Top, and stalagMites point upwards like Mountains!

Glossary

Atmosphere A thick layer of gases around the Earth

Acidic rainwater Rain that contains pollution is often acidic, and it can dissolve rocks and kill plants over time

Atom Tiny building block that makes up all stuff

Bacteria Tiny living organisms that are everywhere, but are too small to see without a microscope

Chemical weathering When rocks are slowly dissolved by acid in rainwater

Core The centre of our planet

Crust The solid, rocky top layer of our planet

Crystal A lump of mineral with naturally flat sides and sharp edges

Deposition A gradual build up of bits of rock

Earthquake Shaking of parts of the Earth's surface

Erosion When rocks are slowly worn away by wind or water

Extrusive rock Rock formed when lava cools and solidifies on the Earth's surface

Facet The flat side of a cut gemstone

Fossil The remains of a living thing, preserved in rock

Fossilise To become a fossil

Geologist A scientist who studies rocks

Horizon The word for the layers in soil

Igneous Rock formed when molten rock solidifies

Impermeable rock Rock that does not soak up water

Intrusive rock Rock formed when molten rock solidifies underneath the Earth's surface

Lava Molten rock that flows on the Earth's surface

Lava bomb A drop of molten rock that flies out of a volcano and solidifies in the air

Mantle The layer of the Earth between the core and the crust

Metamorphic Rock that is formed when another type of rock is put under heat and pressure

Mineral A naturally occurring solid that has the same arrangement of atoms all the way through

Opaque Does not let light through

Palaeontologist A scientist who studies fossils

Parent rock The type of rock a metamorphic rock has changed from

Permeable rock Rock that can soak up water

Properties The characteristics of a rock

Rock A solid material made of a mix of minerals

Rock cycle How rocks are being constantly changed into new types of rock

Sediment Little bits of rock that get deposited on the ground or on lake and ocean beds

Sedimentary Rock that is made of layers of sediment crushed together

Soil erosion When the healthy top layer of soil gets washed away

Tectonic plate Giant jigsaw-like piece of the Earth's crust

Volcano An opening in the Earth's crust where molten rock can escape

Weathering When a rock is broken down on the Earth's surface

Further reading

Earth Cycles: Rock Cycle
Jillian Powell (Franklin Watts, 2014)

Earth Rocks: Metamorphic Rocks
Richard Spilsbury (Wayland, 2016)

Earth Rocks: Minerals
Richard Spilsbury (Wayland, 2016)

Moving Up With Science: Rocks and Soil
Peter Riley (Franklin Watts, 2015)

Websites

www.soils4kids.org
Learn about soil with experiments and games.

www.sciencekids.co.nz/geology.html
Read all about rocks and fossils.

www.bbc.co.uk/education/topics/z9bbkqt
Watch videos about rocks and fossils.

www.rocksforkids.com
For kids of all ages who love rocks.

Index

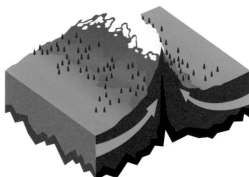

Earth and Space

- What is space? • All about stars and galaxies • What is the solar system? • All about the Sun • All about the Earth • How does the Earth move? • All about the Moon • How does the Moon move? • What is an eclipse? • All about the planets • What are asteroids and comets? • All about space travel

Living things

- What is a living thing? • How are living things grouped? • What is a habitat? • All about food chains • Producers, predators and prey • The life cycle of a mammal • The life cycle of an amphibian • The life cycle of an insect • The life cycle of a bird • All about reproduction • What is evolution? • Our changing environment

Electricity

- What is electricity? • Where does electricity come from? • What do we use electricity for? • All about static electricity • Electrical current and circuits • Conductors and insulators • All about batteries • Electricity and magnetism • How do we make electricity? • All about renewable energy • How do we measure electricity? • Powering circuits

Rocks

- What are Rocks? • All about our rocky planet • What are igneous rocks? • What are sedimentary rocks? • What are metamorphic rocks? • All about the rock cycle • All about erosion and weathering • What are the properties of rocks? • All about fossils • All about soil • What are precious stones? • Amazing rocks

Forces

- What is a force? • Forces around us • What is gravity? • What is magnetism? • All about friction • What is air resistance? • What is water resistance? • All about upthrust • All about elasticity • Balanced and unbalanced forces • All about pressure • Making forces bigger

Sound

- What is sound? • Sound on the move • Loud and soft • Sound and hearing • What is an echo? • Blocking sound • Ultrasound and infrasound • Animal hearing • What is music? • Recording sounds • Sound and science

Light

- What is light? • Sources of light • Light on the move • Light and materials • What are shadows? • What is reflection? • What is refraction? • Colourful light • Light and sight • Light and life • Types of light • Light and health

States of Matter

- Materials and matter • States of matter • All about solids • All about liquids • All about gases • Melting and freezing • Evaporating, boiling and condensing • The water cycle • What is a mixture? • Separating mixtures • Permanent state changes • The future of materials